Mind, Spirit, Science: A Journey of Personal Transformation

2024
Amari Rise Publishing
3315 San Felipe Rd #97 San Jose Ca 95135
www.amaririse.com

Table of Contents

Foreword: An Invitation to Transformation

In a world filled with constant change, uncertainty, and moments of pain, we seek something unchanging to anchor our lives. *Mind Spirit Science: A Journey of Personal Transformation* is a guide for those longing for growth grounded in biblical truth. Through scripture, reflection, and personal stories, this book offers more than advice—it provides a pathway to real, lasting transformation rooted in faith.

This journey is about embracing the power of God's promises, trusting Him in every season, and allowing His word to renew our hearts and minds. As you walk through each chapter, may you discover the strength and resilience that come from leaning into God's love, and may His promises sustain you, guiding you to live with purpose, hope, and unwavering faith.

Introduction: A Journey that Began with Faith

This book is born from my life's journey—a journey shaped by faith, resilience, and countless lessons in trusting God. Growing up, I never imagined the paths I would take, the mountains I would climb, or the valleys I would pass through. Yet, through it all, God was with me, guiding me even when I couldn't see the way forward.

Life has brought me both blessings and battles. From raising six wonderful children to facing the end of a marriage I thought would last forever, I have learned that God's love and strength never fail. Moving from California to Atlanta and now to Florida, I found myself in a new season of life—one of quiet reflection and a deeper relationship with God.

In this season, I have discovered that true transformation comes from the inside out. It's not about changing our circumstances but allowing God to change us through His word. Just as He promises in **Romans 12:2**, we are transformed by the renewing of our minds. This book is my journey and my heart—a sharing of the scriptures, practices, and reflections that helped me walk through life's challenges with grace and faith.

In *Mind Spirit Science*, you'll find a path to personal growth, filled with practical tools and spiritual truths to help you on your journey. My hope is that, as you read, you'll find comfort in knowing that God walks with you too, ready to transform your heart and guide you in every season. So take a deep breath, trust in His love, and let the journey begin.

Opening Thoughts: Grounding in Faith

Transformation is at the heart of the Christian journey. In a world filled with challenges and uncertainties, we seek growth not through our own strength but through the renewing power of God. This book, *Mind Spirit Science: A Journey of Personal Transformation*, is a guide to experiencing deep, lasting change by anchoring ourselves in biblical truths and allowing God's wisdom to guide our steps.

Scriptural Foundation:
Romans 12:2 serves as the cornerstone of our journey:
"Do not conform to the pattern of this world, but be transformed by the renewing of your mind. Then you will be able to test and approve what God's will is—his good, pleasing, and perfect will."
Through this verse, we are reminded that true transformation happens when we surrender our thoughts and actions to God, allowing Him to reshape us into His image.

Life Experience:
Reflecting on my own journey, I've seen firsthand how God's word can guide us through life's most challenging moments. There was a time when I felt overwhelmed by the weight of my circumstances. Instead of finding answers in external solutions, I

found strength in Romans 12:2, meditating on the power of renewing my mind. This simple but profound shift—looking to God for direction—became the foundation of my transformation. Through each step, I learned to lean on scripture as a source of strength and guidance.

Purpose of the Book:

This book is a tool for anyone who wants to walk in the purpose God has set for them. Each chapter will explore how biblical principles can help us build resilience, emotional wisdom, and a life filled with gratitude and purpose. It's about letting God's word shape us, trusting that He has a unique and powerful journey planned for each of us.

Chapter 1: Foundations of Transformation in Christ

Opening Reflection:

True transformation begins with a foundation rooted in Christ. Our journey to personal growth and resilience isn't about relying on our own strength but about leaning into God's promises. The Bible teaches us that, in Christ, we are new creations, constantly being renewed and strengthened. It's through this divine process that we can overcome challenges, build resilience, and live purposefully.

Scriptural Foundation:

A powerful scripture that defines our foundation in Christ is **2 Corinthians 5:17**:

"Therefore, if anyone is in Christ, he is a new creation. The old has passed away; behold, the new has come."

This verse reminds us that, as believers, we are made new in Christ. Transformation is not a one-time event but a continual journey, an ongoing renewal as we grow closer to God.

Building Resilience Through Faith:

When we face difficulties, the Bible encourages us to draw strength from God. In **Philippians 4:13**, we are reminded:

"I can do all things through Christ who strengthens me."

Whether we're facing a personal setback or a challenge in our relationships or careers, this verse serves as an anchor. Through Christ, we gain resilience—not because we are strong, but because He is.

Life Experience:

During a particularly challenging season of my life, I felt overwhelmed and unsure of where to turn. Through my prayer and study, **Philippians 4:13** kept surfacing, reminding me that I didn't have to carry my burdens alone. I began to trust that, with God's strength, I could overcome the obstacles before me. Each day, I repeated this verse, letting it become a source of courage and changes in your outlook or sense of peace. This practice builds a foundation of resilience, grounding you in God's word as you navigate life's challenges.

Conclusion of Chapter 1: resilience. This daily practice transformed my outlook and helped me see challenges as opportunities to grow in faith.

The Power of Faith-Filled Thinking:

God calls us to renew our minds, letting go of limiting beliefs and focusing on His promises. **Isaiah 26:3** speaks to this:

"You will keep in perfect peace those whose minds are steadfast, because they trust in you."

By centering our thoughts on God's faithfulness, we experience peace, resilience, and clarity. This peace is a foundation that strengthens us from within, helping us to rise above the chaos and distractions of the world.

Practical Exercise:

Each day, take time to meditate on a scripture that speaks to your current struggles or needs. Reflect on verses like Philippians 4:13 or Isaiah 26:3, asking God to fill your mind with His truth. Write down your reflections and note any

Building our lives on Christ's foundation equips us to face life with confidence and strength. The world may shift and change, but God's word is steadfast. With this foundation, we can continue on our journey of transformation, knowing that we are never alone, and our strength is renewed daily through Him.

Chapter 2: The Mind and Spirit – Renewing Through Faith

Opening Reflection:

Transformation isn't only about external changes; it starts with renewing our mind and spirit. The Bible emphasizes the power of our thoughts and how our inner life shapes our actions, perspectives, and even our peace. As we choose to focus on God's truths and let go of negative or limiting beliefs, we create space for God's peace to enter our hearts.

Scriptural Foundation:

Romans 12:2 provides a powerful guide for mental and spiritual renewal:

"Do not conform to the pattern of this world, but be transformed by the renewing of your mind. Then you will be able to test and approve what God's will is—his good, pleasing and perfect will."

This verse reminds us that our thoughts and mindset have the power to transform us. By choosing to renew our mind with God's word, we align ourselves with His will and purpose.

Embracing Peace through Scripture:

God's word tells us that we can find true peace by focusing our thoughts on Him. **Isaiah 26:3** highlights this beautifully:

"You will keep in perfect peace those whose minds are steadfast, because they

trust in you."

When we center our thoughts on God's promises rather than on fear or worry, we experience a supernatural peace. This peace protects our hearts and minds, helping us navigate challenges with confidence.

Life Experience:

In my journey, there was a season when worry consumed my thoughts. I realized that my focus had drifted from God's promises to my own fears. Isaiah 26:3 became a source of strength for me. I made it a daily practice to meditate on this verse and remind myself to trust in God's goodness. Slowly, I felt His peace take root in my life, grounding me and easing my worries. This process of refocusing my mind helped me see challenges not as obstacles but as opportunities for faith.

Practical Steps for Renewing the Mind:

To renew our minds, we must actively choose thoughts that align with God's word. **Philippians 4:8** guides us on where to direct our focus:

"Finally, brothers and sisters, whatever is true, whatever is noble, whatever is right, whatever is pure, whatever is lovely, whatever is admirable—if anything is excellent or praiseworthy—think about such things."

This scripture reminds us to focus on thoughts that bring life and positivity, rather than those that drain or discourage us.

Exercise for Daily Renewal:

1. **Morning Meditation**: Start each day by reading a verse that speaks to you. Write it down and reflect on what it means to you personally.

2. **Redirecting Thoughts**: When a negative or anxious thought enters your mind, counter it with a scripture that provides truth and encouragement. Examples could include Philippians 4:13 ("I can do all things through Christ who strengthens me") or Psalm 23:1 ("The Lord is my shepherd; I shall not want").

3. **Evening Reflection**: End each day by reflecting on moments where you felt God's peace or guidance. Write down a verse that resonates and pray for continued renewal.

Conclusion of Chapter 2:

Renewing our mind is an ongoing journey that draws us closer to God, deepening our peace and resilience. By filling our minds with His truths and promises, we develop a spirit grounded in faith rather than fear. This renewed mindset transforms how we see the world and empowers us to live out God's purpose each day.

Chapter 3: Building Emotional Resilience Through the Word

Opening Reflection:

Life's challenges can test our faith, but through God's word, we can find the strength and resilience needed to endure. The Bible offers countless examples of those who, through reliance on God, overcame seemingly insurmountable obstacles. By turning to scripture during difficult times, we develop a spiritual resilience that allows us to face adversity with hope and trust in God's faithfulness.

Scriptural Foundation:

James 1:2-4 provides a powerful perspective on trials and resilience:

"Consider it pure joy, my brothers and sisters, whenever you face trials of many kinds, because you know that the testing of your faith produces perseverance. Let perseverance finish its work so that you may be mature and complete, not lacking anything."

This verse encourages us to see challenges as opportunities for growth. God uses trials to strengthen our faith, helping us build endurance and maturity.

Drawing Strength from God's Promises:

When we face hardships, it's natural to feel overwhelmed, but

God promises to be with us. **Isaiah 41:10** is a comforting reminder of His presence and support:

"So do not fear, for I am with you; do not be dismayed, for I am your God. I will strengthen you and help you; I will uphold you with my righteous right hand."

This verse reassures us that we don't have to face our struggles alone. God is our strength, lifting us up and helping us move forward, no matter the obstacle.

Life Experience:

During one of the most challenging periods of my life, I found myself clinging to Isaiah 41:10. It was a verse I read over and over, letting its truth sink into my heart. As I navigated my struggles, I prayed and reminded myself that God was upholding me. This experience taught me that resilience is not about relying on my strength but about leaning on God's promises and allowing Him to carry me through.

Practical Steps for Building Resilience:

Scripture is our guide to perseverance and emotional strength. **Philippians 4:6-7** encourages us to turn to God in times of worry:

"Do not be anxious about anything, but in every situation, by prayer and petition, with thanksgiving, present your requests to God. And the peace of God, which transcends all understanding, will guard your hearts and your

minds in Christ Jesus."

Through prayer, we bring our fears and concerns to God, allowing His peace to fill us and strengthen us from within.

Exercise for Resilience-Building through Prayer and Scripture:

1. **Identify Your Source of Strength**: When faced with a challenge, turn to a scripture that reminds you of God's faithfulness. Write it down, memorize it, and repeat it in times of need.

2. **Practice Gratitude in Prayer**: Take a moment each day to thank God for something in your life, even during difficult times. This helps shift your focus from fear to trust.

3. **Journal Your Journey**: At the end of each week, write down moments where you felt God's strength and peace. Reflect on how His word has impacted your resilience.

Conclusion of Chapter 3:

Emotional resilience isn't about facing trials alone; it's about finding strength in God's promises. By rooting ourselves in His word and trusting Him, we can endure hardship with peace and confidence, knowing that He is working in us and through us. As we grow in resilience, we become living testimonies of His grace and strength.

Chapter 4: Living Out Faith – Gratitude, Generosity, and Purpose

Opening Reflection:

Living a life of faith isn't just about what we believe—it's about how we live. The Bible calls us to show our faith through gratitude, generosity, and a purposeful life that reflects God's love and grace. As we let our actions align with His word, we become a source of light and encouragement to others, glorifying God in all we do.

Scriptural Foundation on Gratitude:

The Bible encourages us to embrace gratitude in all circumstances. **1 Thessalonians 5:18** reminds us:

"Give thanks in all circumstances; for this is God's will for you in Christ Jesus."

Gratitude is a powerful practice that shifts our focus from our struggles to God's faithfulness, allowing us to see His blessings even in difficult times.

Life Experience in Gratitude:

There was a time when I faced a period of uncertainty, and gratitude felt challenging. But by focusing on small blessings each day, I found myself more grounded in God's presence and less weighed down by worry. I realized that gratitude isn't about ignoring difficulties but about recognizing God's hand in our lives, no matter the season.

Scriptural Foundation on Generosity:

God calls us to give freely and joyfully. **2 Corinthians 9:7** says: *"Each of you should give what you have decided in your heart to give, not reluctantly or under compulsion, for God loves a cheerful giver."* Generosity is more than just financial; it's about giving our time, love, and resources to serve others. When we give, we reflect God's character and open our hearts to His blessings.

Life Experience in Generosity:

One of the most impactful experiences in my life was when I volunteered my time to help those in need. Through these small acts of kindness, I felt a deep connection to God's purpose for me, and I realized how generosity blesses both the giver and the receiver. Giving, especially when done joyfully, brings us closer to God's heart.

Scriptural Foundation on Purpose:

Each of us is created with a unique purpose. **Jeremiah 29:11** reminds us of God's plan for our lives: *"For I know the plans I have for you," declares the Lord, "plans to prosper you and not to harm you, plans to give you hope and a future."* Embracing this purpose means trusting that God has placed us here for a reason, and by seeking His guidance, we find meaning and direction in all we do.

Living Purposefully Through Faith:

Living with purpose involves aligning our actions with God's will. **Proverbs 3:5-6** gives us a simple but powerful approach:

"Trust in the Lord with all your heart and lean not on your own understanding; in all your ways submit to him, and he will make your paths straight."

When we rely on God and seek His guidance, our lives become purposeful, filled with direction and fulfillment.

Exercise for Living Out Faith:

1. **Daily Gratitude Practice**: Begin each day by thanking God for three specific blessings in your life. Reflect on how these blessings show His love and faithfulness.

2. **Acts of Generosity**: Find a way to give each week, whether it's your time, resources, or words of encouragement to someone in need.

3. **Prayer for Purpose**: Ask God to reveal His purpose for you, especially in areas where you feel uncertain. Reflect on scriptures like Jeremiah 29:11 and Proverbs 3:5-6 as you seek His guidance.

Conclusion of Chapter 4:

Living out our faith through gratitude, generosity, and purpose deepens our relationship with God and positively impacts those around us. By focusing on these virtues, we create a life that honors Him, allowing us to fulfill the unique purpose He has for each of us. As we continue this journey, let us remember that every act of faith, no matter how small, is a step closer to living the abundant life God has promised.

Chapter 5: Conclusion – Embracing God's Plan

Opening Reflection:

As we reach the end of this journey, we're reminded that personal transformation is not a single event but a lifelong process of growing closer to God, trusting His promises, and aligning our lives with His purpose. Every chapter in this journey of faith builds on the foundation of God's love, grace, and guidance, equipping us to face life's challenges with resilience and hope.

Scriptural Foundation for God's Plan:

God's promises are at the heart of our journey, assuring us that we are never alone. **Proverbs 16:9** reminds us:

"In their hearts humans plan their course, but the Lord establishes their steps."

While we may have our own plans and goals, it's God who ultimately directs our path. Embracing His plan means surrendering our desires, trusting that His purpose for us is greater than anything we could imagine.

Living with Faith and Trust in God's Timing:

In times of uncertainty, it's easy to feel anxious about the future. But God calls us to trust Him fully, even when we don't understand the full picture. **Romans 8:28** offers a powerful reminder:

"And we know that in all things God works for the good of those who love him, who have been called according to his purpose."

This verse teaches us that every experience, whether joyful or challenging, can be part of God's greater plan for our lives.

Life Experience of Trusting God's Path:

In my own journey, I've encountered moments where I didn't understand why certain doors were closed or challenges arose. But as I continued to place my trust in God, I saw how He used those moments to shape me, to grow my faith, and to lead me to places I hadn't anticipated. Each step reminded me of the importance of trusting in His timing and His purpose.

A Call to Faithful Living:

As we step forward, let us commit to living a life of purpose and faith, knowing that we are continually being shaped by God.

Proverbs 3:5-6 encapsulates this trust perfectly:

"Trust in the Lord with all your heart and lean not on your own understanding; in all your ways submit to him, and he will make your paths straight."

By surrendering our lives to God, we invite His guidance and assurance, knowing that He has a perfect plan for each of us.

Final Exercise: A Prayer of Surrender

Take a moment to reflect on God's purpose for your life and how He has shaped you through your experiences. Write a prayer of surrender, asking Him to lead you in the areas where you seek guidance and thanking Him for the journey of growth and resilience you've undertaken.

- *Example:* "Lord, I trust in Your purpose for my life. I surrender my plans to You, knowing that Your wisdom is greater than mine. Guide me each day and help me to live out Your will with joy, resilience, and gratitude. Amen."

Closing Thought:

Transformation is a journey that unfolds one step at a time. By embracing God's word, seeking His guidance, and trusting in His promises, we become a living testament to His faithfulness. As we continue forward, may we find strength in His love, peace in His presence, and purpose in His promises.

Epilogue: A Life Held by God

My life has been a journey of transformation, one marked by both trials and the grace that sustains me. Reflecting back, I see how God has shaped me through every season, each filled with challenges and growth. As a mother of six and a grandmother, I've experienced the deep joys and the heartaches that come with raising a family. I faced my hardest battles—like the end of my marriage—with God as my constant support. Through it all, He was my rock and my comfort.

Leaving California to start anew in Atlanta, and then moving again to Florida, each transition was a step of faith. Now, as I embrace this season of life, I find myself in a quiet place—a single life, an empty nest. It's just me and God. In this solitude, I feel His presence more intimately than ever. It's here I find peace, knowing He has always been my provider and promise-keeper.

Through the scriptures, I've come to understand resilience, gratitude, and the strength of faith. **Philippians 4:13** reassures me, *"I can do all things through Christ who strengthens me."* When I could have lost my mind to pain, He kept my mind secure. Just as He promised in **Deuteronomy 31:6**, God has never left me nor forsaken me.

This book, *Mind Spirit Science*, is a testament to that journey. It's an epilogue to *Be Still*, a continuation of faith, resilience, and hope. Even in moments when I thought I had lost everything, God showed up, healing wounds I never thought would close. As I look forward, I do so with the assurance that God has a purpose for me, and I embrace whatever He has in store. In Him, I find my identity, my purpose, and my peace.

Made in the USA
Columbia, SC
23 November 2024

46984385R10015